DATE DUE			

GREAT RIVER REGIONAL LIBRARY

St. Cloud, Minnesota 56301

GAYLORD M2G

San Diego

San Diego

A Downtown America Book

Karen O'Connor

Dillon Press, Inc. Minneapolis, MN 55415

Library of Congress Cataloging-in-Publication Data

O'Connor, Karen.
  San Diego / Karen O'Connor.
    p.   cm. — (A Downtown America book)
  Summary: Describes the past and present, neighborhoods,
historic sites, attractions, festivals, people, industries, climate,
and social problems of San Diego.
  ISBN 0-87518-439-1 (lib. bdg)
  1. San Diego (Calif.)—Juvenile literature. [1. San Diego
(Calif.)] I. Title. II. Series.
F869.S22026   1990

                                                    CIP
                                                    AC

Dillon Press, Inc., 242 Portland Avenue South
Minneapolis, Minnesota 55415

Printed in the United States of America
1 2 3 4 5 6 7 8 9 10 99 98 97 96 95 94 93 92 91 90

To Jane Graham and Maria Morris
with love and appreciation.

Acknowledgments

Special thanks to Gail Sonora and Maria Morris
of the Greater San Diego Chamber of Commerce,
Laurie De Selms of the San Diego Convention and
Visitors Bureau, Mayor Maureen O'Connor, Carole
O'Connell, and Lynn Gunner for their assistance.

Our appreciation to James Blank for the photos
used in this book. Additional photos have been pro-
vided by the San Diego Historical Society, and the
Port of San Diego. Cover photo by James Blank.

Contents

City Flag.

City Seal.

Fast Facts about San Diego

San Diego: America's Finest City; The Birthplace of California

Location: Southern California coast; the southwestern corner of the United States, bordered on the south by Mexico, and on the west by the Pacific Ocean

Area: City, 319.6 square miles (827 square kilometers), including 72.7 square miles (189 square kilometers) of water; county, 4,255 square miles (11,020 square kilometers)

Population (1989 estimate*): City, 1,086,600; consolidated metropolitan area, 2,418,200

Major Population Groups: Whites, Hispanics, African Americans, Asians

Altitude: 20 feet (6 meters) above sea level

Climate: Average temperature in January is 55°F (13°C); in July, 70°F (21°C); average annual precipitation, including rain, melted snow, and other moisture is 10 inches (25 centimeters)

Founding Date: 1769; incorporated as a city in 1850

City Flag: The red, white, and yellow flag includes the city seal and the date, 1542, when explorer Juan Rodríguez Cabrillo sailed into the San Diego Bay

City Seal: A shield within a circle, crowned with a bell tower which is a symbol of the influence of the missionaries on the city's early development

Form of Government: Council-manager; voters elect a mayor and eight other city council members to four-year terms; the council appoints a city manager to serve as administrator of the government

Important Industries: The military, aerospace, entertainment, tourism, shipbuilding, agriculture, electronic and oceanographic equipment, medical research

Festivals and Parades

January: Martin Luther King, Jr. Day Parade

February: Oceanside Whale Festival

March: Ocean Beach Kite Festival; St. Patrick's Day Parade

April: Southwest Indian Festival; Pacific Beach Spring Festival; Day at the Docks

May: Campland on the Bay Jazz Festival; Peninsula Arts Festival; Cinco de Mayo Festival; Spring Village Faire; Ethnic Food Fair

June: Del Mar Fair; La Jolla Festival of the Arts; Indian Fair; Greek Festival; San Diego Scottish Highland Games

July: Independence Day celebrations; Sand Castle Days; Festival of the Bells; Mission San Luis Rey Fiesta; Caribbean Day Fest; Sports Fiesta

August: California State Games Festival; Latin American Festival; Barona Indian Mission Fiesta; Hillcrest City Fest

September: Underwater Film Festival; International Seafood Fair; Adams Avenue Street Fair; Cabrillo Festival

October: Harvest Festival and Christmas Crafts Fair; Zoo Founders Day; Columbus Day Parade; Ye Olde English Faire

November: El Cajon's Mother Goose Parade; Thanksgiving Dixieland Jazz Festival; North Park Toyland Parade

December: Christmas on the Prado; Wild Animal Park's Festival of Lights; Old Town Christmas Parade; San Diego Harbor Parade of Lights; Holiday in the City Parade

For further information about parades and festivals, see agencies listed on page 56.

United States

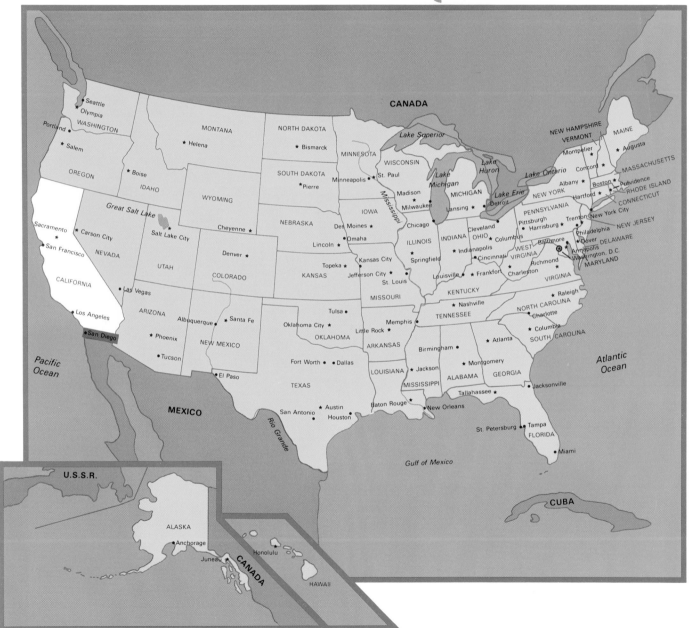

San Diego

CALIFORNIA

San Diego●

ESCONDIDO

Cleveland National Forest

DEL MAR

SAN DIEGO FREEWAY

CABRILLO FREEWAY

San Diego

Torrey Pines State Reserve

⑪

La Jolla

Miramar Naval Air Station

SAN DIEGO RIVER

EL CAJON

Pacific Beach

Mission Beach

MISSION BAY

Mission Valley

⑧

⑩

⑨

⑥ ⑦

Mission Bay Park

Balboa Park

①

ⓝ

N

④ ②

③

North Island Naval Air Station

San Diego Naval Station

⑤

Point Loma

SAN DIEGO BAY

CHULA VISTA

Points of Interest

① San Diego Zoo
② Community Concourse
③ Horton Plaza
④ Star of India
⑤ Cabrillo National Monument
⑥ Old Town
⑦ Serra Museum
⑧ Sea World Aquarium
⑨ San Diego State University
⑩ Mission San Diego de Alcalá
⑪ Scripps Institution of Oceanography
⑫ San Diego Wild Animal Park

PACIFIC OCEAN

UNITED STATES

MEXICO

TIJUANA

| 0 | miles | 5 | 10 | 15 |
| 0 | kilometers | 5 | 10 | 15 | 20 |

⑫

1

America's Finest City

"San Diego feels good all over!" This familiar slogan appears on bumper stickers and billboards throughout San Diego. Most residents of this beautiful southern California city agree, and would not think of living anywhere else.

San Diego is located on San Diego Bay in the southwestern corner of the United States. The Pacific Ocean lies to the west and the Laguna Mountains to the east. Camp Pendleton, a naval base, lies to the north, while San Diego's southern border is shared with Mexico.

San Diego residents can shop in nearby Tijuana, Mexico, hike in the mountains, study wildflowers in the desert, surf in the ocean, or sail on the bay. San Diego Bay is considered one of the world's finest deepwater harbors. This has made the city one

The Laguna Mountains rise behind San Diego Bay and the downtown area.

of the nation's chief naval and aircraft centers.

The bay and the harbor are also excellent places for recreation. Restaurants, hotels, and campgrounds surround the bay. A short distance from the harbor is beautiful Balboa Park, home of the San Diego Zoo. The park also contains museums, art galleries, and nature exhibits.

The greater San Diego area includes the city of San Diego and the surrounding communities in San Diego County. More than 70 square miles (182 square kilometers) of inland water and sunwashed beaches lie within the county's borders. About 1 million people live in the city, while 2 million live throughout the county.

San Diego is one of the fastest growing major cities in the United States. In 1989, it passed Detroit, Michigan, to become the sixth largest metropolitan area in the country. In California, only Los Angeles is larger.

More than 90 percent of San Diego's permanent residents were born in the United States. The Hispanic community makes up about 15 percent of the population, while African Americans make up 6 percent. As Hispanics continue to cross the border from neighboring Mexico, Spanish is fast becoming the city's second language. The population also includes people from Great Britain, Canada, Europe, Asia, and Africa.

One reason all these people come to San Diego is its climate.

San Diegans sail near Point Loma.

Average temperatures range from 55°F (13°C) in winter, to 70°F (21°C) in the summer. The warm, sunny weather makes San Diego a popular vacation spot, attracting visitors from all over the world. Within the city's borders, it is possible to hear French, Portuguese, Arabic, German, Chinese, and Japanese.

By 2000, Asians and Hispanics will most likely be the largest population groups in San Diego. People with European backgrounds are expected to become the minority.

The different ethnic groups in the city bring with them different values and customs. These are seen in the growing number of churches and temples. Roman Catholics form the largest religious group in San Diego. There are also large numbers of Jews, Protestants, and members of various Eastern religions.

Finding new and better means of transportation for the growing population is a problem for city leaders. Today, it is not difficult to travel around the city by bus or car because of the freeway system that crosses through the main areas of San Diego County. In coming years, however, experts believe traffic jams could be common sights as more people visit and move to the area. Developers are planning ways to avoid these problems.

The San Diego Trolley, the San Diego-Coronado Ferry, and the Harbor Hopper are three of the newest ways to travel in San Diego. Shuttles

Balboa Park is a popular place to go roller skating.

and tour buses, too, offer visitors and residents quick transportation from one location to another.

San Diego also moves people by air and rail. Lindbergh Field is used by 18 airlines, while 60 steamship lines dock in the harbor. Railroad lines, for both freight and passengers, also pass through San Diego.

Most people, though, don't remember San Diego for its transportation. They remember San Diego for its stately palm trees, pounding surf and ocean breezes, deep canyons, spectacular cliffs, and sparkling beaches. Is it any wonder that residents consider their hometown "America's Finest City"?

The Pacific Ocean surf pounds against rocky cliffs in northern San Diego.

2

The Birthplace of California

In 1542, Juan Rodríguez Cabrillo sailed into San Diego Bay. He may have been the first European to see the area. Before that, the coast was home to the Diegueño Indians. Cabrillo was actually a part of a group of Spanish explorers. They were searching for a shortcut to China!

Sixty years later, Sebastian Vizcaino brought another expedition to San Diego. On November 12, 1602, the Spanish explorer named the area *San Diego*, in honor of a Spanish priest, San Diego de Alcalá.

The Spanish, however, did not try to settle there for another 167 years. In 1769, Father Junípero Serra, a Franciscan missionary, arrived in San Diego from Mexico City. With him was Gaspar de Portolá, a Spaniard. Portolá established a *presidio*—a military fort—to protect San

Mission San Diego de Alcalá, the first California mission.

Diego's port. Within the walls of the presidio, Father Serra built California's first mission.

San Diego became a Mexican *pueblo* (town) in 1834 when Juan Maria Osuna was elected its first mayor. But in 1848, following the Mexican-American War, the town came under the control of the United States.

Within 10 years, San Diego grew from 140 to several hundred people. Early residents included American soldiers and sailors who came to the town during the war. They joined the original Mexican settlers.

Gradually, people from the East Coast moved to the West. Stage coach lines and overland mail routes drew more people. By 1854, San Diego was large enough to receive an official United States lighthouse. It was built on Point Loma, near the entrance to San Diego Bay.

On April 15, 1867, one of the city's most important developers arrived by steamer. Alonzo E. Horton had heard about the wonderful opportunities in San Diego. After surveying the town, though, he decided it was in the wrong location. He quickly purchased 1,000 acres (400 hectares) of land near the harbor for $265.

Horton built a 100-room hotel—Horton House—a new wharf, and many other new buildings. He also gave plots of land to investors. As the new San Diego rose alongside the harbor, the old town crumbled from lack of use.

Point Loma lighthouse was built in 1854.

Alonzo E. Horton.

In 1885, the California Southern Railroad reached San Diego and created a land boom. New businesses opened, and thousands of people moved west. By the spring of 1888, though, the business boom was finished. The European stock market had crashed, and a terrible flood struck the city. Many people had to sell their property to pay their debts. Ten thousand people moved out of San Diego, leaving street after street of deserted houses.

John D. Spreckles, a millionaire from northern California, rescued the city. He built a new wharf, and became a major investor in city buildings, newspapers, and theaters. The Spreckles Theater—"the finest theater in the West"—brought fine arts

to San Diego. Spreckles also gave the city its first railroad across the mountains to the east.

In 1915, The Panama-California Exposition opened in what is now Balboa Park. City officials planned it after the opening of the Panama Canal in 1914. Thousands of visitors flocked to the city for this celebration.

Between 1914 and 1918, many jobs were created when Fort Rosecrans was built on North Island. Franklin D. Roosevelt, then secretary of the navy, had recommended the fort after visiting San Diego for the exposition in 1915. In 1922, the Eleventh Naval District opened its headquarters in San Diego.

At the other end of the city, Dr. Harry Wedgeforth was busy developing another kind of project. He had started the city's first zoo. Wedgeforth began with a small collection of animals left behind after the 1915 exposition.

In 1927, San Diego became well known after Charles Lindbergh's flight across the Atlantic Ocean. The Ryan Aeronautical Company of San Diego had built his monoplane. Eight years later, the city received more attention when the Consolidated Aircraft Corporation—now Convair—moved there. Also in 1935, the city hosted its second fair.

During World War II, San Diego grew and changed rapidly. The city's airplane plants attracted thousands of workers from all over the United

States. The U.S. Navy, Army, and Marine Corps built new military bases in the city. Following the war, many of the navy and other military personnel returned to San Diego to live and work.

During the early 1950s, tuna fishing made San Diego the leading fishing port in the country. By the late 1950s, the city had a major shipbuilding industry. San Diego companies also began building weapons for the U.S. military. The city later became known for its marine research at the Scripps Institution of Oceanography in La Jolla.

In 1961, San Diego built its first stadium. Three years later, the San Diego campus of the University of California (UCSD) opened.

During the 1970s, Mission Valley, the land below Father Serra's first mission, became a successful business center. New office buildings and modern malls drew shoppers, tourists, and businesspeople away from the crowded downtown area. San Diego County grew to 1.5 million.

Toward the end of the 1970s, people began paying more attention to the old downtown area. The turn-of-the-century buildings in the Gas Lamp Quarter were restored to their original appearance. Nearby shops were cleaned up and redecorated.

On the site of the old Horton House now stands a huge, multi-level shopping mall called Horton Plaza. This modern building is a bold and colorful blend of Italian, Victorian,

With dozens of shops and restaurants, Horton Plaza is a popular meeting place for San Diegans.

Seaport Village is a re-creation of an old harbor community.

and Spanish architecture. Like its neighbor, Seaport Village, Horton Plaza provides hundreds of jobs and brings millions of dollars into the city each year.

With all these changes, however, came problems. Today, pollution, crime, gang wars, illegal aliens, and drugs are some of the city's biggest challenges. Cocaine and other illegal drugs enter San Diego from Mexico and South America. San Diego is sometimes called the "crack" capital of the United States.

To deal with these problems more effectively, schools have developed anti-drug programs for students. The Border Patrol—which polices the Mexican-American border—and the San Diego Police Department are increasing their forces. Public and private groups offer help to people with drug problems.

Homelessness is another of the city's most pressing concerns. From 3,000 to 5,000 homeless adults and children live in cars and on the streets. They sleep on benches, under bridges, and along the beach.

Part of the city's new development plan includes low-rent hotels and apartments for people with low or fixed incomes. Some programs are already underway. In southwest San Diego, for example, Father Joe Carroll has opened a large, modern, long-term shelter for homeless families. Also, since 1983, parents and children have been coming to the Saint Vincent de Paul/Joan Kroc Center. They can live here for as long as two years while they learn job skills, find work, and save money for a future home.

For many years, people recognized San Diego only for its beauty. Today, though, the area is becoming known for all it has to offer—sound business ideas, medical and military research, quality education, and a caring population.

3

At Home in San Diego

The colors and styles of San Diego homes are like a patchwork quilt. Orange-tiled roofs dot the hillsides of Rancho Bernardo. Colorful Victorian homes line the streets of Golden Hill. Mexican-style houses cling to the hillsides overlooking La Jolla Shores.

Despite the differences in their homes, most San Diego residents share a love of outdoor living. That is no surprise. According to the United States Weather Bureau, 300 out of 365 days are rain-free in San Diego!

Hot tubs and swimming pools are popular additions to homes with large yards. Greenhouse windows, sunrooms, wood decks, and tile patios allow residents to enjoy the sunshine year-round. Many of the new, "planned communities" in San Diego include a swimming pool, tennis

Turrets and detailed trim are typical of Victorian houses like this one in San Diego.

High-rise condominiums and apartment buildings on the coast of Coronado, a San Diego area community.

courts, a golf course, and a neighborhood park.

Most San Diegans have a variety of housing styles and neighborhoods to choose from. People who serve in the military, however, do not have as many choices. The city has a serious shortage of housing for people in the U.S. Navy and other armed forces. Many enlisted men and women are forced to leave their families behind and live in singles quarters when they are transferred to San Diego. The navy plans to improve housing for at least one-third of service families. As of 1990, though, no new units had been added.

Some members of the armed forces, as well as working and retired people, live in downtown San Diego.

Here, they are close to transportation, shopping, offices, and the waterfront. New high-rise condominiums and apartment buildings are replacing old, run-down structures. Also, many single rooms to rent or own for people who live alone are making the downtown area a desirable place to live and work.

Throughout the year, downtown San Diego is a popular place to celebrate everything from Saint Patrick's Day to the Fourth of July. For the Annual Street Scene, the historic Gas Lamp Quarter changes into a lively neighborhood party with jazz, African, cajun, and rock music.

Each year, the downtown area is also the setting for the colorful Columbus Day Parade, the Harvest

Outdoor cafes and specialty shops are common in the Gas Lamp Quarter.

Festival and Christmas Crafts Market, and the Holiday in the City Parade. In mid-December, people gather downtown for the annual San Diego Harbor Parade of Lights. Colorfully lit boats glide across the downtown harbor after nightfall.

Located a few miles north of downtown is the Old Town district, the original center of the city. Today, the Mexican village is a collection of shops, restaurants, a theater, mission churches, and historic homes.

Most Old Town residents live in single-family cottages. At least 25 of the families living in Old Town have lived there for more than 50 years.

Old Town is a special attraction for San Diego schoolchildren. Each Monday morning, groups of fourth graders from various city schools gather at Fremont School and then tour the village to learn about the history of their city. On Friday of the same week, they celebrate their "graduation" by presenting a play about the arrival of Father Junípero Serra.

"Living History" is another children's program in Old Town. It is offered the first Saturday morning of each month. Students in grades one through six learn to bake bread, plant vegetables, shape adobe bricks, and make candles just as children did 150 years ago.

People from all over San Diego come to Old Town for a variety of parades and festivals. The fun-filled Mexican celebration, Cinco de Mayo, occurs in May. In July, visitors and

Colorful homes surround Heritage Park in Old Town.

residents enjoy an old-fashioned Fourth of July celebration. During the Christmas holiday, the colorful Old Town parade features high school bands, clowns, horse riders, and antique cars.

On the bluffs above Mission Valley and Old Town, neighbors celebrate some interesting and unusual festivals. City Fest is held each August. This outdoor art exhibition and festival honors Hillcrest, one of San Diego's older communities. Residents of nearby North Park present a Toyland parade each November. The celebration includes food, games, and free llama rides for children.

San Diegans can also enjoy the food and folklore of different cultures. The Southwest Indian Festival, Greek Festival, and San Diego Scottish Highland Games are held each year in various parts of the city.

To the north of Mission Valley are the family communities of Linda Vista ("Pretty View"), Clairemont, and Mira Mesa. These neighborhoods have a mix of low-rent apartments, modern condominiums, and neat, older homes with shade trees. The residents are of a variety of ethnic backgrounds. They include Vietnamese, Hispanics, African Americans, and native Americans. To the north of these neighborhoods lies an area known as the "Golden Triangle." Here, research centers, major shopping malls, and high-rise office buildings and hotels attract people from all over the city.

Across from Mira Mesa is the old Scripps Ranch property. It is now home to large, modern houses and condominiums. The neighborhood spreads across hills and canyons and is surrounded by towering eucalyptus trees. The Scripps Ranch Fourth of July celebration draws neighbors together for an old-fashioned community parade and picnic.

For those who prefer beach living, there are a number of small communities along the ocean. From the tip of Point Loma, where San Diego was founded, to the shores of La Jolla, there is a neighborhood to suit almost everyone.

Ocean Beach, Mission Beach, and Pacific Beach are older communities. Their residents range from surfers and university students, to families and retired people. Most homes in the area were built in the 1930s and 1940s. New condominiums and apartments are gradually replacing some of the older houses.

Beach residents can get together for a number of festivals and celebrations. The Pacific Beach Christmas Parade, the Spring Art Festival, and the Ocean Beach Kite Festival are just a few of the more popular celebrations.

Point Loma's Christmas Home Tour and Cabrillo Festival attract people from all over the city each year. The festival honors Cabrillo's discovery of the West Coast in 1542. It features a band concert, Portuguese, Mexican, and American dancers, and ethnic food booths.

La Jolla ("The Jewel") is still one of the most impressive of all San Diego communities. The jagged coastline, hilly streets, canyon views, and charming village shops combine the best San Diego has to offer. Residents celebrate Christmas with a community parade and party. Street banners, marching bands, floats, and craft displays make it a colorful celebration.

From downtown to La Jolla, every city neighborhood has schools. More than half of the school district's students are minorities. Because of this, San Diego schools try to teach about the different cultures and peoples that make up the city. Five universities and several colleges provide higher education for both residents and students from across the country. The University of California and San Diego State University are the most well known.

Whether they live in a beach home or a downtown condominium, San Diego residents take a special pride in their city. Just as many colorful squares make up a patchwork quilt, the different neighborhoods and people of San Diego combine to create a colorful and exciting city.

Neighbors take part in building a giant sand castle at Pacific Beach.

4

From Trading to Tourism

San Diego business is rooted in the land. Before the area was discovered by explorers, native Americans grew a variety of crops along the shores of San Diego Bay. They used these crops to trade for food, clothing, and shelter.

Today's San Diego residents still enjoy the natural gifts of the land. Produce stands, ranch wagons, and farm trucks set up shop along coun- try roads and city corners. Some even pull into shopping malls for a Saturday morning Farmer's Market.

Trees, shrubs, plants, and flow- ers are the most important agricul- tural products in the county. Local nurseries provide everything needed to landscape a front yard, plant a window garden, or decorate an apart- ment terrace.

Today, agriculture is San Diego's

These fields of flowers are an important part of the agriculture industry in San Diego.

fourth largest industry. In California, the county remains the largest producer of avocadoes and tomatoes. San Diego is also one of the top 20 agricultural counties in the United States.

Manufacturing, the military, and tourism—in that order—are the three major industries in San Diego. Like agriculture, each began during the city's early days.

Widespread manufacturing began during World War II when airplane and shipbuilding companies opened in the city. The mild climate and open spaces created the perfect location for huge aircraft factories and year-round test flights. San Diego Harbor was an ideal spot for building and testing ships and seaplanes.

By 1942, 45,000 people were at work manufacturing parts for ships and planes.

Today, much of the city's manufacturing is still related to military needs. But during the 1980s, high technology products began replacing some of the defense manufacturing.

Aerojet General, for example, is developing an exciting new superfast engine that will allow airplanes to travel from coast to coast in 45 minutes. Rohr Industries is one of the leading manufacturers of jet engine *nacelles* (the pod-shaped objects that cover aircraft engines).

A new and important development for San Diego industry is the rise of *maquiladoras*. Maquiladora is the term for twin-plant operations between the United States and Mexico. American business owners agree to open branches of their companies in Mexico. Organizers hope this will reduce the number of Mexicans who cross the border illegally in search of jobs. In 1988, more than 400 maquiladoras were in business.

One of the most exciting items manufactured in San Diego is the CRAY X-MP/48 supercomputer. This superfast computer was developed at UCSD. X-MP/48 can make 840 million calculations per second. It will be used in future space program systems.

The military is one of San Diego's biggest employers. The county is home to one of the largest naval stations in the world and the largest marine training center in the United States.

The different military branches provide jobs for nearly 200,000 people—both servicepeople and civilians. This is more than any other industry in the city. Almost two-thirds of San Diego's manufacturing business comes from federal government contracts for defense weapons and aerospace equipment.

There are 101 ships based in San Diego. Three of these are aircraft carriers: the U.S.S. *Constellation*, the U.S.S. *Ranger*, and the U.S.S. *Independence*. Each carrier is like a small city. One of these ships requires more than 5,000 military and hundreds of non-military workers to keep it running.

A U.S. Navy ship decked out in colorful banners waits at Broadway Pier.

Navy ships attracted worldwide attention in 1988 when San Diego-based crews patrolled the seas in the Persian Gulf. These ships showed the important role San Diego plays in the nation's military affairs.

San Diego is a favorite place for military men and women to retire. Nearly 50,000 retired personnel live in the county—the highest such number in the nation.

San Diego is also a community respected for its medical research and development. The UCSD Medical Center, Scripps Memorial Hospital, and the Salk Institute attract skilled doctors, nurses, researchers, and other medical professionals from around the world.

Finance and world trade are also

important to the San Diego business community. The International Division of the Greater San Diego Chamber of Commerce helps businesses that export goods to Mexico, Canada, and the Asian nations along the Pacific Rim.

Perhaps the best-known source of business in San Diego is tourism. Thousands of people in this field work so that others may play. Whether they are driving a tour bus at the zoo or managing a dolphin show at Sea World, workers in the tourism industry of San Diego serve more than 30 million visitors each year.

Elisha S. Babcock may have started it all back in 1885 when he decided to build a grand hotel in Coronado. The Hotel Del Coronado, known as "The Del" to locals, has drawn guests from many nations.

More than 100 years after the Del was built, the San Diego Convention Center opened on San Diego Bay. This world-class waterfront center hosts international trade shows and conventions.

In other parts of the city, tourism provides jobs in hotels, restaurants, theaters, parks, museums, theme parks, shopping centers, and historic sites. High school and university students often work part-time in the tourism business as waiters and waitresses, hotel clerks, cashiers, tour guides, and salespeople. Many begin full-time work in the same business when they finish their education.

San Diego is also a town that encourages the small businessowner. More than 70 percent of the companies in the area have 50 employees or less. It is a city of opportunity for people with creative ideas—people such as Louise Howten.

In 1978, Louise Howten opened The White Rabbit, a bookstore featuring only children's books. At that time, it was the only one of its kind, and few people believed it could be successful. Since it opened, though, it has served as an example to more than 300 children's bookstores across the country.

From its small family farms to its giant aircraft manufacturers, San Diego's industries combine the best of the past and the future. In this way, San Diegans hope to be ready for the changes to come in the next century.

The Hotel del Coronado attracts politicians, celebrities, and tourists from around the world.

5

San Diego at Play

Visitors are not the only ones who have fun in San Diego. For many residents, living in San Diego is like being on vacation year-round. From the beginning, city developers saw the importance of setting aside land for play and relaxation.

Alonzo E. Horton not only shaped the industry of San Diego, he also shaped the recreation. Horton dreamed of building a beautiful park in the center of town. His dream became a reality in 1879, when Balboa Park was built.

Today, Balboa Park consists of more than 1,000 acres (400 hectares) of plants, grass, trees, and natural canyons. It is a place of great fun for children as well as adults. Young people can ride an old-fashioned carousel and a miniature railroad. Summer visitors enjoy Marie Hitchcock's

Visitors to Balboa Park can take advantage of more than a dozen museums, as well as acres of gardens and open spaces.

puppet shows, as well as classes and workshops at the Reuben H. Fleet Space Center.

Located at the north end of Balboa Park, the San Diego Zoo is the city's most famous attraction. Here, young people can visit the Children's Zoo, featuring an animal nursery and petting zoo. Adults and children enjoy the entertaining animal shows that are offered daily.

For the look and feel of an African safari, there is the Wild Animal Park, located 30 miles (48 kilometers) north of downtown San Diego. From a monorail, visitors watch wild animals roam free in large, open spaces.

San Diego is also a popular spot for water sports. As early as 1902, city officials saw the need for beach and picnic areas along the coast. Mission Bay Park is a result of their planning. It is a 4,600-acre (1,840-hectare) beach playground, the largest of its type in the world. Sailing, fishing, swimming, surfing, and board sailing are the most common activities on the 27 miles (43 kilometers) of sparkling beaches.

World-famous Sea World is also located on Mission Bay. Marine life exhibits, the popular Penguin Encounter, Killer Whale Skywalk, Shamu Stadium, and the new Places of Learning offer both fun and information. Included in the price of admission is Cap'n Kid World, a kids-only playground.

San Diego Bay is another popular

The giraffe exhibit at world-famous San Diego Zoo.

The *Star of India*, a 100-year-old sailing ship, is docked permanently in the San Diego harbor.

attraction. For a look at San Diego's sailing history, visitors can walk to the nearby Maritime Museum. Exhibits include the century-old sailing ship, the *Star of India*, and other historic sea vessels.

The Cabrillo National Monument and the Old Point Loma Lighthouse are located at the tip of Point Loma, where Juan Rodríguez Cabrillo landed in 1542. This scenic spot offers a sweeping view of San Diego's harbor and coastline. It is also one of the best places to watch the

California gray whale as it travels to its breeding grounds.

For a taste of the past, San Diegans visit Old Town. Here, some of San Diego's original buildings, such as Casa Bandini, still stand. Casa Bandini was the home of one of the city's first residents. It is now a popular Mexican restaurant. Other early adobe and wood frame buildings have been turned into shops, cafes, and museums.

One of Old Town's favorite spots for shopping and eating is Bazaar Del Mundo ("World Bazaar"). While there, many children stop at the Mexican bakery for a *churro* (fried sweet roll) or *pan dulce* (sweet bread). Others choose a homemade *tortilla* (a thin cornmeal pancake) stuffed with chopped meat or cheese and *frijoles* (beans) at one of the Mexican cafes.

Old Town is located at the base of a hill. At the top is Presidio Park and the Serra Museum, site of the city's first presidio and mission. Mission San Diego de Alcalá in the valley below still holds services every Sunday in the original chapel.

San Diego also has something to offer youngsters who want a mountain and desert experience. There are hundreds of miles of hiking trails in nearby Cleveland National Forest and in the Anza-Borrego Desert to the east. Local trails and a nature museum are located in La Jolla at Torrey Pines State Reserve.

Sports fans will feel at home in

San Diego. Horse racing, tennis and golf, sky diving, hot air ballooning, bicycling, swimming, surfing, and water skiing are just a few of the activities San Diegans enjoy. Residents can also watch the San Diego Chargers play professional football and the Padres play baseball at the San Diego Jack Murphy Stadium.

Young athletes in San Diego can get their start through the city's Department of Parks and Recreation. Programs for children in basketball, softball, soccer, and other sports are offered regularly.

Scripps Aquarium, the art museum, and the natural history museum also offer programs, classes, and field trips especially for children. The city has its own Children's

The bright flowers and beautiful fountains of *Bazaar del Mundo.*

Museum for young people fourteen and under. Here, children can take part in special exhibits and events. They can pretend to be a news broadcaster or produce skits on stage.

San Diego young people can learn about their city's symphony, opera, theater, and zoo without leaving their schools. These groups often sponsor programs through local schools. There are also two cultural groups especially for children—the San Diego Youth Symphony and the San Diego Junior Theatre.

Holidays in San Diego are a special time for children. Each year on the Sunday before Thanksgiving, the nearby community of El Cajon features the Mother Goose Parade. Floats, bands, clowns, horses, and the famous Mother Goose characters delight children of all ages.

Today, the San Diego Zoo, Balboa Park, Old Town, and other attractions are great places to visit. But more importantly, they link the modern city with the pueblo of the past. As San Diego moves toward an exciting future, these places remind residents and visitors alike of San Diego's rich history.

Places to Visit in San Diego

Balboa Park

Information Center
House of Hospitality
1549 El Prado
(619) 239-0512

Aerospace Historical Center
2001 Pan American Plaza
(619) 234-8291

Marie Hitchcock Puppet Theatre
Palisades Building
(619) 466-7128

Museum of Photographic Arts
1649 El Prado
(619) 239-5262

Museum of San Diego History
1649 El Prado
(619) 232-6226

Old Globe Theatre
Simon Edison Center for the
Performing Arts
(619) 239-2255

Reuben H. Fleet Space Theater
and Science Center
1875 El Prado
(619) 238-1233

San Diego Hall of Champions
1649 El Prado
(619) 234-2544

San Diego Junior Theatre
Casa del Prado, Room 208
(619) 239-1311

San Diego Model Railroad Museum
1649 El Prado
(619) 696-0199

San Diego Museum of Art
1450 El Prado
(619) 232-7931

San Diego Museum of Man
1350 El Prado
(619) 239-2001

San Diego Natural History Museum
1788 El Prado
(619) 232-3821

San Diego Youth Symphony
Casa del Prado
(619) 233-3232

San Diego Zoo
2920 Zoo Drive
(619) 234-3153

Starlight Bowl
2005 Pan American Way
(619) 544-7827

Special Interest Museums

Cabrillo National Monument
Point Loma and Catalina Blvd.
(619) 557-5450

Children's Museum
8657 Via La Jolla Dr.
La Jolla Village Square
(619) 450-0767

Firehouse Museum
1572 Columbia Street
(619) 232-FIRE

Junípero Serra Museum
2727 Presidio Drive
Presidio Park
(619) 297-3258

Maritime Museum
1492 North Harbor Dr.
(619) 234-9153

Scripps Aquarium-Museum
Scripps Institution of Oceanography
8602 La Jolla Shores Drive
(619) 534-6933
(619) 534-FISH

Special Places

Bonnie Marie Dance Studio
Coronado Victorian House
1000 Eight St., Coronado
(619) 435-2000

Hotel Del Coronado
1500 Orange Avenue
Coronado
(619) 435-6611

Mission Basilica San Diego de Alcalá
10818 San Diego Mission Road
(619) 281-8499

Old Town State Park
Juan and Taylor streets
Old Town
(619) 237-6770
Home of the "Living History" Program

San Diego Symphony
1245 7th Avenue
(619) 699-4205

San Diego Wild Animal Park
15500 San Pasqual Valley Rd.
Escondido
(619) 747-8702
(619) 234-6541

Sea World of California
1720 South Shore Rd.
Mission Bay
(619) 226-3901
(619) 222-6353

Nature Attractions

Anza-Borrego State Park
Visitor Center
Anza-Borrego Desert
(619) 767-4205

Cabrillo Tide Pools
Cabrillo National Monument
Tip of Point Loma
(619) 293-5450

Additional information can be obtained from these agencies:

Greater San Diego Chamber of Commerce
The Chamber Building
110 West C Street, Suite 1600
San Diego, CA 92109
(619) 232-0124

San Diego Convention and Visitors
Bureau
1200 Third Avenue
San Diego, CA 92101
(619) 232-3101

San Diego: A Historical Time Line

1542   Juan Rodríguez Cabrillo sails into San Diego Bay

1602   Spanish explorer Sebastian Vizcaino names the area San Diego de Alcalá

1769   Father Junípero Serra establishes the first California mission, San Diego de Alcalá

1834   San Diego becomes a Mexican town

1848   San Diego comes under control of the United States

1855   The original Point Loma Lighthouse is completed

1876   New Town is founded by Alonzo Horton

1885   The California Southern Railroad comes to San Diego

1915   The Panama-California Exposition opens

1922   The Eleventh Naval District sets up headquarters in San Diego

1935   Consolidated Aircraft Corporation opens in San Diego; the California-Pacific International Exposition is held

1956   Torrey Pines city park becomes California State Park Reserve

1961   Jack Murphy Stadium opens

1964   The San Diego campus of the University of California opens

1970s   Mission Valley develops into a commercial center

1980s   Downtown San Diego is restored; San Diego trolley opens rail transit to Tijuana, Mexico

1989   New San Diego Convention Center opens; San Diego replaces Detroit, Michigan, as the nation's sixth largest metropolitan area

Index

About the Author

Karen O'Connor has long been fasci-
nated by San Diego. As a resident of
the city, she has seen it grow and
change while maintaining its natural
beauty and unique spirit. Once an ele-
mentary school teacher, Ms. O'Connor is currently a free-lance author,
seminar leader, and writing instructor.
She is the author of more than 20 children's books and over 300 articles
and stories for juvenile publications,
many of which have earned awards.